Facts About
Deserts

DONNA BAILEY

STECK-VAUGHN
LIBRARY
Austin, Texas

How to Use This Book

This book tells you many things about places called deserts and the wastelands of the world. There is a Table of Contents on the next page. It shows you what each double page of the book is about. For example, pages 6 and 7 tell you "How Deserts Are Made."

On some of these pages you will find words that are printed in **bold** type. The bold type shows you that these words are in the Glossary on pages 46 and 47. The Glossary explains the meaning of some words that may be new to you.

At the very end of the book there is an Index. The Index tells you where to find certain words in the book. For example, you can use it to look up words like wadis, dunes, permafrost, and many other words to do with deserts.

Published in the United States in 1990 by Steck-Vaughn Co., Austin Texas, a subsidiary of National Education Corporation.

© Macmillan Publishers Ltd 1989
Artwork© BLA Publishing Limited 1988

All rights reserved. No reproduction, copy or transmission of this publication may be made without written permission.

Material used in this book first appeared in Macmillan World Library: *The Waste Lands.*
Published by Macmillan Children's Books

Printed and bound in the United States
1 2 3 4 5 6 7 8 9 0 LB 94 93 92 91 90

Library of Congress Cataloging-in-Publication Data

Bailey, Donna.
    Deserts / Donna Bailey.
        p.   cm. — (Facts about)
    Summary: Describes various aspects of deserts, including their creation, modernization, plant and animal life, mineral and oil resources, and how humans live there.
    ISBN 0-8114-2511-8
    1. Desert ecology—Juvenile literature. 2. Deserts—Juvenile literature. [1. Desert ecology. 2. Deserts. 3. Ecology.] I. Title. II. Series.   89-26120
QH541.5.D4B35   1990   CIP
574.5'2652—dc20   AC

Contents

Introduction

All over the world there are huge
areas of wasteland called deserts,
where almost nothing lives.

Some places are very hot and dry,
like the Kara Kum Desert in the Soviet
Union, in this picture.

4

There are cold deserts around the North and South Poles, on the waste-lands of the Arctic and Antarctica. These deserts are always covered by snow and ice and the water is frozen.

Scientists visiting Antarctica to work there travel over the snow on **snowmobiles** which have tracks that bite into the snow instead of wheels.

How Deserts Are Made

wind

PACIFIC OCEAN

Rocky Mountains

Deserts are places where there is not enough water for plants to grow.

Rock paintings in the Sahara show that thousands of years ago, people kept cattle that fed on grass. When the **climate** changed the grass and cattle died, and the Sahara became a sandy desert.

rock paintings

6

rain falls on the slopes of the Rocky Mountains facing the Pacific Ocean

rain shadow desert

When winds blow over the oceans they pick up drops of water that form clouds. When the winds reach the land, rain from the clouds falls on the mountain slopes near the ocean.

By the time the winds have blown inland they are very dry, so no rain falls. The land on the other side of the mountains becomes a **rain shadow desert.**

In Antarctica snow falls from clouds and the wind blows it into snowdrifts.

Antarctic snowdrifts

Water and Wind

Some deserts are covered with sand,
some with rocks or stones.

Weather can change the **landscape** of
a desert over thousands of years.
Rain falls heavily in fierce storms.
It washes away the top layer of soil
and **erodes** the rocks underneath,
making dry valleys called **wadis.**

sand dunes in the Sahara

**this wadi in Morocco may
stay dry for months or years**

rocks eroded by wind

Tiny grains of sand blown by the wind have carved these huge pillars of rock in the Navajo Desert in Arizona.

In the Sahara, wind blowing sand across the desert makes huge **dunes**. Some dunes in the Sahara are 1,300 feet high. They change their shape and size as the wind changes its direction.

Plants in Hot Deserts

Plants like the desert poppy have **adapted** to live without much water.

  After a heavy storm, the desert poppy bursts into flower. It soon dies but leaves behind seeds that will grow when it rains again.

Mexican poppy

desert poppy

carpet of snow

Other plants, like the
cactus, store water in
their leaves or stems.
After a storm, the cactus
soaks up water through its
giant roots and stores it
in its thick, fleshy stem.
The cactus uses the water
it stores to grow bigger.

saguaro
cactus

barrel
cactus

aloe

Wildlife in Hot Deserts

All desert animals must be able to
live with very little water.
They find ways of keeping cool in the
burning desert heat.

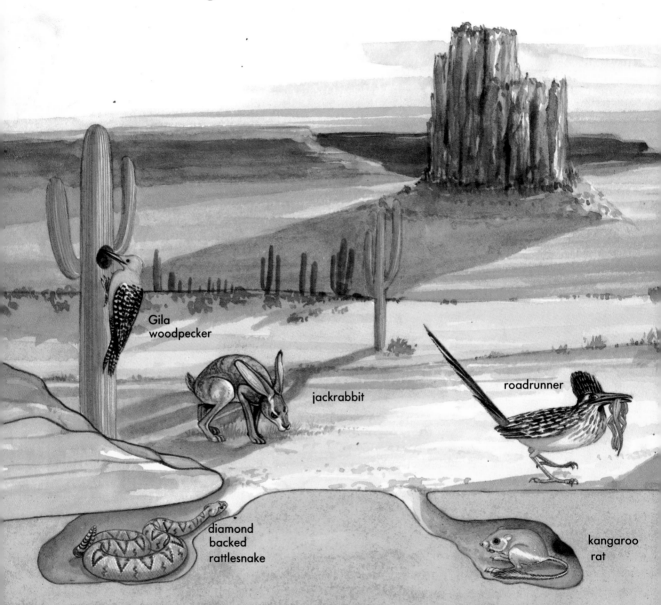

Gila
woodpecker

jackrabbit

roadrunner

diamond
backed
rattlesnake

kangaroo
rat

Lizards and snakes shelter in burrows
between rocks or under plants.
Other animals dig burrows too, and
come out at night to look for food.
They must look out for **predators** like
the sparrow hawk and the kit fox.

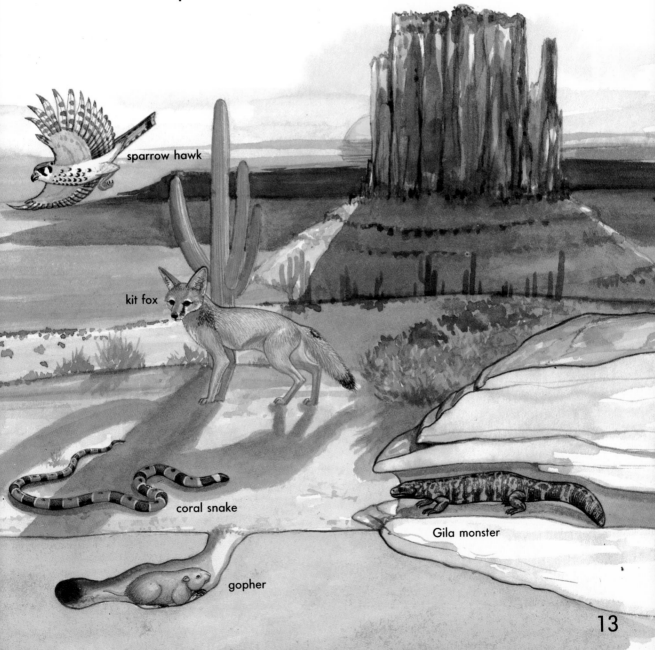

sparrow hawk

kit fox

coral snake

Gila monster

gopher

The Tundra

The tundra is a cold, mostly flat area of land between the Arctic ice cap and the tree line of Greenland, North America, Europe, and the Soviet Union. The winters are long and cold. Snow covers the ground, which is frozen solid three feet below the surface and is called **permafrost.**

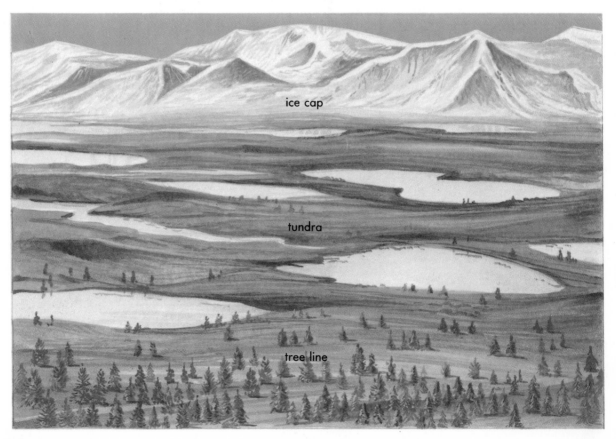

ice cap

tundra

tree line

flowers on the tundra

The snow melts for a few weeks in the short summer. The ground is wet and boggy and the tundra is covered with flowers that die but leave new seeds. Lichens and mosses, which can stay alive under the snow, cover the rocks. Grasses and heathers grow on flat, stony ground.

lichens and mosses

Wildlife in the Tundra

The animals that live in the tundra have adapted to keep warm during the cold winter months.
The arctic fox has a thick **pelt** and tufts of hair inside its ears to help keep it warm.

Musk oxen roam the tundra in herds, finding mosses and lichen to eat under the snow which they scrape away with their hooves. Musk oxen and caribou both have broad hooves to help them move easily over the soft snow.

a caribou's hoofprint (left)

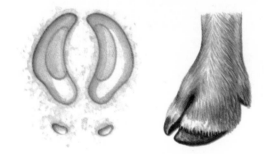

a musk ox's hoof (right)

The shaggy coats of musk oxen hang down to their hooves and keep them warm.

To protect their calves against cold winds and predators, musk oxen stand in a circle around them.

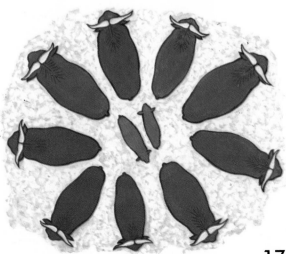

17

The Polar Deserts

narwhals

polar bear

walrus

harbor seals

The deserts of the North and South Poles
are the coldest areas on Earth.

The Arctic is a large frozen ocean
surrounded by the most northern lands of
North America, Europe, and the Soviet Union.

Polar bears live in the Arctic and feed
on seals and young walruses. Narwhals
feed on the fish they find in the waters
around the **pack ice.**

Antarctica is a **continent** made up of frozen land surrounded by sea.

Animals and birds stay close to the Antarctic coast, where the seas are full of fish and **plankton.**

Penguins catch the fish, and whales and seals eat the fish and plankton.

No one lives in Antarctica except scientists, who go there to study the wildlife and the weather.

Water in the Hot Desert

People living in the desert need water for drinking and cooking. Most water comes from the sudden rain storms, but in some places, water from underground rocks comes to the surface in springs, water holes, or wells.

People take the water to the village in clay jars.

an artesian well

Sometimes wind power is used to pump water up to the surface.

The water from the **artesian well** in the picture is stored in tanks.

collecting water in clay jars

In some parts of the desert, water
from rocks far below the ground is
forced up to the surface through
cracks in the rocks to make an **oasis.**
The water allows crops to grow which
provide food for the desert animals.

The people at the Moroccan oasis in
our picture have built a town nearby.
They use water from the oasis to
grow date palms and other crops.

Living in the Desert

Most people who have adapted to life in the desert are **nomads.** They move from place to place to find water.

The San people of the Kalahari Desert hunt wild animals and gather plants and roots to eat. They make their shelters from long grass and tree branches.

The San people wear very little clothing. They have few **possessions.** The San have lived this way for hundreds of years.

Other nomads, like the Bedouin of North Africa, have found that their way of life is changing fast.

The Bedouin in the picture lives in a town or village. The falcon he is holding is trained to hunt small birds and desert animals. Many Bedouin have stopped traveling and have become farmers and landowners.

These travelers in the Sinai Desert have frame tents and use jeeps to carry their equipment.

These people are just about to leave their base camp for a trek in the Sinai Desert, Egypt. They use jeeps to carry their frame tents and equipment.

Where Are the Wastelands?

Our map shows the cold tundra lands
that surround the Arctic Ocean.
The coldest **temperature** ever recorded
was -128.5°F at Vostok in Antarctica.

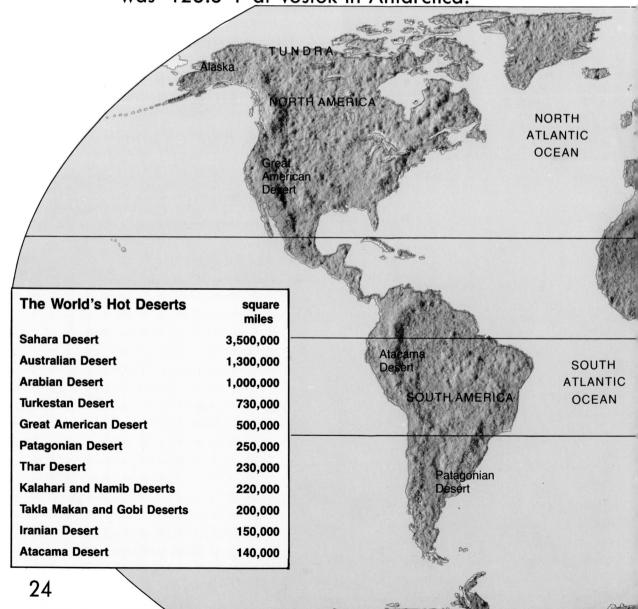

The World's Hot Deserts	square miles
Sahara Desert	3,500,000
Australian Desert	1,300,000
Arabian Desert	1,000,000
Turkestan Desert	730,000
Great American Desert	500,000
Patagonian Desert	250,000
Thar Desert	230,000
Kalahari and Namib Deserts	220,000
Takla Makan and Gobi Deserts	200,000
Iranian Desert	150,000
Atacama Desert	140,000

Many hot deserts stretch across North Africa and the Middle East to the Gobi Desert in central Asia.

The temperature in Death Valley in the U.S.A. once reached 135°F. The driest place in the world is the Atacama Desert in South America.

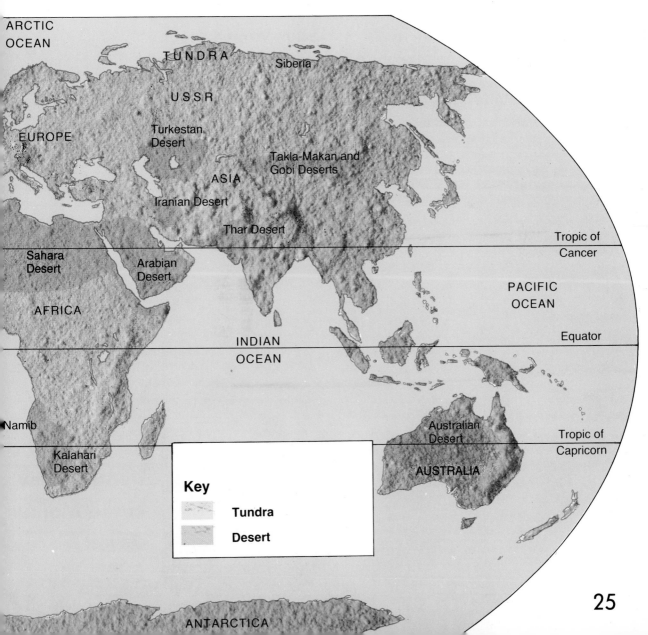

ARCTIC OCEAN

TUNDRA

Siberia

USSR

EUROPE

Turkestan Desert

Takla-Makan and Gobi Deserts

ASIA

Iranian Desert

Thar Desert

Tropic of Cancer

Sahara Desert

Arabian Desert

PACIFIC OCEAN

AFRICA

INDIAN OCEAN

Equator

Namib

Australian Desert

Tropic of Capricorn

Kalahari Desert

AUSTRALIA

Key

Tundra

Desert

ANTARCTICA

Desert Barriers

Deserts act as natural barriers because they are difficult and dangerous to cross.

Over 100 years ago, many people died in the great heat of Death Valley. They had come to this desert in California in search of gold.

Death Valley in the Mojave Desert, California

camels can travel long distances without food and water

Camels have carried people and goods across deserts for hundreds of years. Today trucks are being used more often instead of camels. The truck in our picture is filling up with supplies of water and gasoline.

The Gobi Desert

The cold deserts of central Asia are
the Gobi Desert and the Takla Makan.
The Gobi Desert is a huge desert
covered with sand, gravel, and rocks.
It has hot summers but cold winters.
The Mongol people who travel across
the Gobi Desert are nomadic **herders.**
They use two-humped Bactrian camels
to carry their goods.

These two-humped Bactrian camels are used by
the nomads of the Gobi Desert. The camels'
thick fur keeps out the bitter cold.

The Mongols keep herds of sheep, goats, and yaks. They have to keep the herds on the move in search of fresh grass.

They get milk, butter, cheese, and meat from their animals, and make clothes from woolen cloth and sheepskins.

Mongols live in round tents called **yurts,** but now many of them live in **settlements,** like the one in our picture at Ulan Bator in Mongolia.

29

The Outback

Most of central Australia is a huge wasteland called the Outback.
It is largely covered with **scrub,** which is made up of eucalyptus and acacia trees.

The animals living in the Outback, like these gray kangaroos, are only found in Australia.

The Aborigines were the first people to live in Australia. They adapted to life in the desert.

Aborigines make patterns and paintings that have special hidden meanings. The man in our picture is painting a wooden shield.

Today many people work in the **mines** in the Australian desert. Iron, copper, and lead are mined from the hills around Mount Isa, which is the town shown in our picture.

Bringing Water to the Desert

Water can be brought to dry desert
land by **irrigation.**

Water from a nearby river is held
back by a **dam** to make a **reservoir.**
The water from the reservoir is
pumped along pipes to the dry land.
The water is sprayed evenly over the
land by irrigators, which move along
the fields watering the crops.

soft rock

hard rock

an artesian well

Some irrigators have a long arm that moves around in a huge circle to water the land.

Water held underground between layers of hard rock can be brought to the surface by artesian wells.

crops watered by irrigation grow well

Oil from the Desert

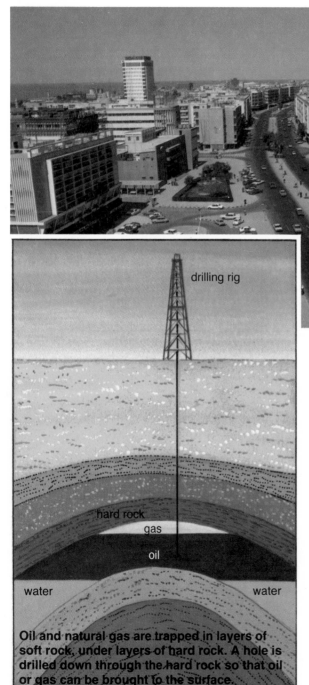

drilling rig

hard rock

gas

oil

water

water

Oil and natural gas are trapped in layers of soft rock, under layers of hard rock. A hole is drilled down through the hard rock so that oil or gas can be brought to the surface.

Kuwait City is built on land that was once desert. Oil under the desert made people in Kuwait rich enough to build a city.

Oil and natural gas are found in underground rock. The drilling rig makes a hole through the rock so the oil or gas can be brought to the surface.

The drilling rig in our picture towers high above the desert in Dubai.

Nearly half the world's oil comes from the Arab states in North Africa and the Middle East.

The oil is sold for high prices to countries that have no oil of their own. Huge tankers take it to many parts of the world.

our diagram shows where the world's supply of oil comes from

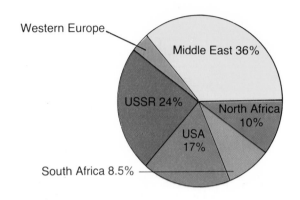

Western Europe
Middle East 36%
USSR 24%
North Africa 10%
USA 17%
South Africa 8.5%

an oil field in Dubai

Minerals of the Desert

Minerals are stones, metals, and kinds of salt. Some minerals are found on the surface of deserts. The Atacama Desert is rich in **nitrates** that are used to help crops grow well.

Some metals, like gold and silver, are **precious metals** and hard to find.

Other metals like iron and copper are used to make things in factories all over the world.

Diamonds and opals are precious stones that are used for jewelry. They are found in hard rocks that the miners must break to get them.

Minerals of the Wastelands						
Deserts	Diamonds	Precious Metals	Iron Metals	Copper	Other Metals	Chemicals
Arabian						●
Atacama			●	●	●	●
Australian		●	●	●	●	
Great American		●	●	●	●	●
Iranian			●			
Kalahari and Namib	●		●	●	●	
Patagonian			●	●	●	
Polar	●	●	●	●	●	●
Sahara			●		●	●
Takla Makan and Gobi			●	●	●	
Thar			●		●	
Turkestan		●	●	●	●	

Bauxite, another useful mineral found
in many of the wastelands, is used
to make a metal called aluminum.
It is used to make parts of cars.

Our picture shows tin mining in Niger.
The tin is near the surface of the
sandy soil so the workers use sieves
to sift it from the sand.

Working in Cold Lands

Our map shows the cold wasteland of Alaska, which is rich in oil. The red line shows the Trans-Alaskan pipeline which carries the oil from the Arctic Ocean to the Pacific Ocean.

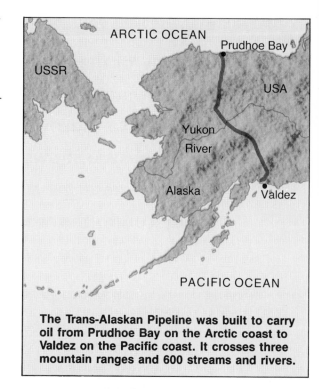

The Trans-Alaskan Pipeline was built to carry oil from Prudhoe Bay on the Arctic coast to Valdez on the Pacific coast. It crosses three mountain ranges and 600 streams and rivers.

working on the Trans-Alaskan pipeline

In winter the temperature in Alaska
can drop to -70°F so workers on
the pipeline must wear warm clothes.

There are many weather stations on
the ice cap, like the one in our
picture, where scientists take
readings of the temperature and wind
speeds to help **forecast** the weather.

The Growing Desert

If the land on the edge of a desert is eaten by too many animals, the grass may not grow back again.
Without grass to protect it, the land will be eroded by wind and rain and will become more desert.

when goats climb trees to feed on the leaves, the trees soon die

In the area to the north of the Sahara, people keep herds of goats that have **overgrazed** the land.

In the Thar Desert in northwest India, animals have stripped the land of most plants. Our picture shows a water hole in the Thar Desert. There is very little food for the animals that are gathered around it.

the Thar Desert

north of the Sahara

Disaster

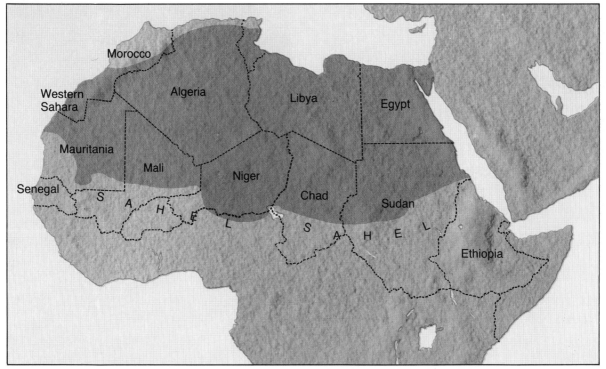

Our map shows the world's worst disaster area, which stretches across Africa from west to east.

Millions of people try to live in the area on the edge of the Sahara Desert called the Sahel. In a **drought,** it, too, becomes desert.

During a drought that lasted four years, 250,000 people and millions of animals died.

children in the Sahel

In recent years drought has brought disaster to parts of Ethiopia and the Sudan, where the crops have failed and many people like these children are **undernourished.** People in other countries have raised money to send help or **famine relief** to feed the starving people.

cows look for water

Ways of Life

The Inuit who live in Alaska used to
be nomads, moving from place to place,
hunting and fishing and living in **igloos.**
Now the Inuit live in wooden huts and
if they need help, or a doctor, a plane
comes quickly to the settlement.
The planes are equipped with skis for
taking off and landing on the snow.

Oil has changed the lives of many Bedouin nomads, who now own farms and send their children to school in the villages.

But desert people still keep some of their old ways of life. At this market in Morocco, the men wear special clothes and sell their goods and spices as they have done for hundreds of years.

Glossary

adapted   changed in order to suit different surroundings.

artesian well   a deep hole in the ground out of which water is pumped.

climate   the weather conditions of an area or country.

continent   a large piece of land that may contain many countries. The Earth is divided into seven continents.

dam   a strong wall built to hold back a river.

drought   a period of time when no rain falls.

dunes   hills of sand built up by the wind.

erode   to wear away the land by the action of ice, water, or wind.

famine relief   help given to people who are suffering from lack of food.

forecast   telling what the weather will be like during the next 24 or more hours.

herders   people who tend flocks of animals.

igloos   houses made of blocks of snow.

irrigation   watering the land using a system of pipes. Water is pumped through from rivers and dams.

landscape   what an area of land looks like.

mines   places where minerals are dug out of the ground.

nitrates   substances added to the soil to help plants grow more quickly.

nomads   people who move from place to place with their homes and animals.

oasis   a place in the desert where water comes to the surface and plants can grow.

overgrazed   when the grass on an area of land has been eaten by too many animals.

pack ice   large pieces of floating ice that drift around in the sea.

pelt   the thick fur and skin of an animal.

permafrost   soil beneath the surface that is frozen all the time.

plankton   tiny animals and plants that float near the surface of the seas and oceans.

possessions   things that are owned and belong to someone.

precious metals   metals used to make expensive jewelry.

predators   animals that hunt and eat other animals.

rain shadow desert desert on
the side of a mountain farthest
from the sea which receives little
rain.

reservoir a large tank or lake
where water is collected and
stored.

scrub low bushes and small
trees that grow on dry land.

settlements places where
people live in groups of buildings
which form towns or villages.

snowmobiles special motorized sleds
for traveling over the snow.

temperature the measure of
heat or cold.

undernourished not having
enough food to keep healthy and
grow properly.

wadis dry valleys or riverbeds
in a desert. When it rains, a wadi
fills very quickly with water and
floods, often killing animals.

yurts round tents made from fur
and skins, used by Mongols in
the Gobi Desert.

Index

Acknowledgments
The Publishers wish to thank the following organizations for their invaluable assistance in the preparation of this book.
British Petroleum
Canadian High Commission
Oxfam
Photographic credits
(t=top b=bottom l=left r=right)
Cover: Robert Harding Picture Library; title page Robert Harding Picture Library; 4 ZEFA; 5 Ed Lawrenson; 6 The Hutchison Library; 7, 8 ZEFA; 8/9 Hans Christian Heap/Seaphot; 9 The Hutchison Library; 15t Canadian High Commission; 15b John Lythgoe/Seaphot; 16 L.H. Newman/NHPA; 17 Stephen Krasemann/NHPA; 19 Jonathan Chester/NHPA; 20t The Hutchison Library; 20b Jeremy Hartley/Oxfam; 21 Douglas Dickens; 22 Peter Johnson/NHPA; 23t The Hutchison Library; 23b Peter Scoones/Seaphot; 26, 27t ZEFA; 27b, 28 The Hutchison Library; 29t, 29b ZEFA; 30 Vincent Serventy/Seaphot; 31t, 31b The Hutchison Library; 32 Hans Christian Heap/Seaphot; 33 ZEFA; 34 The Hutchison Library; 35 British Petroleum; 36, 37 The Hutchison Library; 38 British Petroleum; 39 Ed Lawrenson; 40 Dennis Firminger/Seaphot; 41t ZEFA; 41b Hans Christian Heap/Seaphot; 43t, 43b Jeremy Hartley/Oxfam; 44 ZEFA; 45t The Hutchison Library; 45b Mike Coltman/Seaphot

DATE DUE			

574.5   Bailey, Donna.
B

Deserts.

897699 01596 58358B 10007E